Women
at the Front

Women at the Front

Their Changing Roles in the Civil War

by Jean F. Blashfield

A First Book

Franklin Watts
A Division of Grolier Publishing
New York - London - Hong Kong - Sydney
Danbury, Connecticut

Photos ©: Brown Brothers: 50, 53; Corbis-Bettmann: 11, 15, 24, 27, 29, 30, 34, 35, 36, 44, 45, 48; Culver Pictures: 12, 18, 28, 40 left; Library of Congress: cover, 42; Michael McAfee: 40 right; Museum of the Confederacy: 14; National Portrait Gallery, Smithsonian Institution/Art Resource, NY: 9, 16; North Wind Picture Archives: 20, 55; Schlesinger Library, Radcliffe College: 31.

Library of Congress Cataloging-in-Publication Data

Blashfield, Jean F.
Women at the front: their changing roles in the Civil War/ by Jean F. Blashfield

p.   cm.—(A First book)
Includes bibliographical references and index.
Summary: Explores ways in which the various activities of women during the Civil
    War altered their role in society and led to new initiatives in women's rights.
ISBN 0–531–20275–5
1. United States—History—Civil War, 1861–1865—Women—Juvenile literature.
    2. Women—United States—History—19th century—Juvenile literature.
    [1. United States—History—Civil War, 1861–1865—Women.   2. Women—
    History.] I. Title. II. Series.
E628.B53   1997
973.7'15042—DC20

                                                              96–31319
                                                              CIP
                                                              AC

CONTENTS

Chapter One
Half the Population

The story of the Civil War is not just a story of a young nation in struggle, or even the story of African-Americans acquiring their freedom. It is also the story of women and the great changes that came to them from their participation in and suffering through the war.

During the Civil War, women of both North and South found their lives and their hopes changed. They did much more in the war than defend their homes or wait for their soldiers to come home. They fought. They spied. They nursed the wounded. They supplied the troops. And they kept their own homes going and their children growing at the same time.

FOUR YEARS OF CHANGE

In the mid-1800s, conflicts built up between northern and southern states about the right of each state to

Northern women were generally safe in their homes. But in the South, as here in Atlanta, Georgia, women were often forced by the war to move out of their homes and seek shelter elsewhere.

decide for itself whether its residents could own slaves. After Abraham Lincoln, a Northerner, was elected president of the United States in 1860, southern states began to secede, or withdraw, from the Union.

War between the United States of America, or the Union, and the new nation formed by the seceding states, called the Confederate States of America, or the Confederacy, started in April 1861. Most people thought it would be over in just a few months. It wasn't. America's Civil War lasted four years.

The United States at the time of the war included everything east of the Mississippi River, plus several states west of the river. There were about 15 million women and 16 million men, most in the North. More than 3 million men fought.

Most of what we know of the lives of women who lived through the war is based on the diaries of individual women of the North and South. Louisa May Alcott, who would later write *Little Women,* envied the men she watched going off to fight. She wrote in her diary, "I've longed to be a man; but as I can't fight, I will content myself with working for those who can." Millions of women did the same.

"THE LITTLE LADY WHO STARTED THE BIG WAR"

Harriet Beecher Stowe, daughter of a family of writers, preachers, and teachers, wrote the novel *Uncle Tom's Cabin, or Life Among the Lowly.* It was published in forty-five weekly segments in 1851 in *The National Era,* an antislavery newspaper. Her own child had died in 1849, and she was acutely aware of the anguish that losing a child—whether to disease or the auction block—could bring. Her main character, Uncle Tom, was a gentle man who was sold to Simon Legree, a plantation owner who treated his slaves cruelly.

When published as a book, *Uncle Tom's Cabin* influenced thousands of readers in the North to think about the institution of slavery. In the South, the book was burned.

When the Civil War began, President Abraham Lincoln met Harriet Beecher Stowe. He supposedly said, "So you're the little lady who started the great big war." Stowe's own son, Fred, quit medical school to go to war. He was wounded at Gettysburg and never fully recovered.

Chapter Two
At Home—North and South

Not everyone in the North was enthusiastic about the war at first. Many people thought that the southern states had every right to secede. Others were not very concerned about slavery—especially laboring men who were afraid that African-Americans released from slavery might take their jobs.

When the war started, there were fewer than fifteen thousand soldiers in the U.S. Army. In order to fight a war, the federal government had to call for volunteers. Most towns easily put together companies of volunteer soldiers for the civilian army. More than a million men answered the call to fight for the Union. A third of them would die in this war.

The government did not supply uniforms for any soldiers except those in the standing U.S. Army. Men in the civilian army had to find their own uniforms. Usually

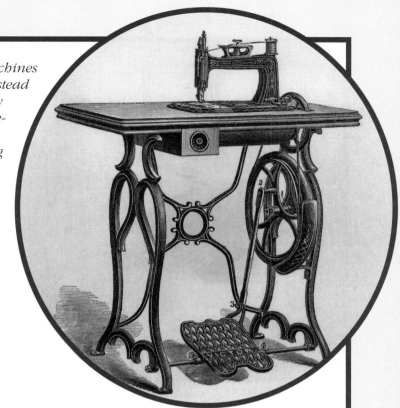

The early sewing machines ran by foot power instead of electricity, but they were a great improvement over sewing clothing and bedding by hand.

they were made by the women, even down to changes of socks and the bedding rolls they carried on their backs. This led to an incredible variety of colors and styles of uniforms.

The sewing machine powered by a foot treadle had been invented in 1849, so it was available for much of the heavy work done by women. A group of women with one such machine could turn out ten times as much work as women sewing by hand.

LIFE IN THE NORTH

Because some people in the North were far from the action of the war, much of life went on as before. Well-to-do people who were used to taking vacations away from home continued to do so. Concerts and theatrical events were still held. Working people continued to go to their jobs, although they made more products for use in the war.

Maryland, a border state, was an important transfer point for moving escaped slaves along the so-called Underground Railroad to safety in the North. Harriet Tubman, an ex-slave, was one of the founders of the escape route from Maryland.

Only rarely did people in the North find war on their doorsteps. In Maryland, a very divided state, Barbara Fritchie defied the order to lower Union flags as Stonewall Jackson's Confederate troops approached the town of Frederick. She waved the United States flag from her rooftop, ignoring the gunshots that zipped toward her from passing troops.

Few battles reached into the North. Those that did, such as Gettysburg, were fought out in the open countryside. The women of the South, on the other hand, faced a war that came right into their homes.

DETERMINED WOMEN OF THE SOUTH

Southerners were not fighting just to defend the practice of slavery. Instead, they were fighting for the right to run their lives as they saw fit, without interference from a federal government. They willingly and quickly put together a whole army eager to take on the North to maintain that right.

It soon became clear, however, that the enthusiasm of volunteers was not going to be enough. The Confederacy passed a law calling for every man between the ages of eighteen and thirty-five to enter the military. This act brought the war home to virtually every mother, daughter, sister, and wife.

Many women were left alone with children to support. Farm wives spent four rugged years doing the man's work of running the farm, the woman's work of feeding and raising the family, and the war work of spinning, weaving, knitting, and rolling bandages. The end

Men left home to fight the war, leaving their wives to raise the children and take care of the farms.

On many farms, women had to plant and harvest the crops while their husbands were at war.

of the war found many southern women exhausted and often quite ill.

When the Union general William T. Sherman captured Savannah, Georgia, he had his men keep a special eye on the women because, as he announced, "You women are the toughest set I ever knew. The men would have given up long ago but for you. I believe you would keep this war up for thirty years."

ONE WOMAN AND HER DIARY

Mary Chesnut was raised in one South Carolina slave-owning, political family and married into another. She was the wife of the first U.S. senator to resign from the United States Congress to help his state secede. Because her husband worked for Confederate President Jefferson Davis, Mary Chesnut was at the center of the political and social arena.

The diary she kept during the war tells of life in Richmond, the capital of the Confederacy. It is a detailed and charming diary, recording personal events and gossip as well as military planning. But it conveys only an upper-class view of the war.

Unlike many Southerners, Mary Chesnut questioned the ethics of owning other people and called herself an abolitionist. But, like many Southerners, she also felt that most slaves were "unromantic, undeveloped savage Africans."

WOMEN AND SLAVES

We sometimes have an image of southern slave-owning women as living quiet, even lazy, lives, while their slaves did all the work. But most of these women were busy from morning to night making sure that everyone on the plantation had clothing, food, and supplies. They made sure each person stayed healthy and was taught what he or she needed to know. Only one in four southern families actually owned slaves—they were too expensive for most.

Slave owners reacted quite differently to the war. Some tried to keep their slaves from discovering that the war was deciding their future. Many women, though, realizing that slavery was at an end, began to teach their slaves to read and write in preparation for freedom.

WORKING FOR THE WAR

Most war-related activities of southern women were of a private nature. Many women gave up meat and other foods that could be used as rations for soldiers. They often became ill with malnutrition. Some women who could do little else wrote letters every week to every soldier they knew, hoping that the letters would help to

Staunch southern women in Middleborough, Virginia, were recorded throwing stones at Union cavalrymen.

encourage and cheer the fighting men.

Until late in the war, any Confederate soldier could expect to be given aid in any southern house he entered. Almost every woman within a hundred miles of a battle site was sent sick or wounded soldiers for her to nurse in her home.

Month by month, as southern funds to continue the war were used up, women dug deeper and deeper into their own treasures to contribute to the cause. Their jewels became cash. They turned their carpets into soldiers' blankets, their silk dresses into observation balloons, and their everyday dresses into men's shirts.

"MAKING DO"

The Union was blocking ships from using southern ports, so southern women were unable to buy new things throughout most of the war. They made do with what they had. They invented substitutes for coffee, such as toasted seeds and burned corn. They made shoes out of squirrel skin or braided straw. They dug up the ground under smokehouses, retrieved the salt used in preserving meat, and then used it again.

Southern women did not stop the entertaining that was so much a part of their lives. They held "starvation" parties, at which everyone dressed up in their finery, but no food was offered. This was the best they could do in the traditionally hospitable South.

INVADERS IN THE HOME

When Union armies moved into a town, they took over the biggest houses as headquarters and housing for offi-

Southern homes were often taken over by Union officers who simply demanded possession of them when a town had been captured.

cers. The women were kicked out, left to fend for themselves and their families as best they could. When word spread that Union soldiers were approaching, some women tried to smuggle items of value out of the house and hide them. They quickly ate food supplies, especially meat, and they buried silver and jewels where they could not be found and stolen.

More terrifying were the freebooters, soldiers of either side who left their regiments and roamed through the countryside, taking whatever they could. They often invaded homes, demanding food, stealing anything of value they could find. They were more likely to harm women than the regular soldiers were.

Many Southerners, terrified of the coming Yankees, fled their homes and towns, carrying what they could. They became refugees in their own land, seeking safety in such places as Texas, Florida, and southern Georgia.

Southern women often showed their contempt for "invading" soldiers from the North by pointedly moving their skirts aside when a soldier walked by (to keep them from being "contaminated"), by calling them names, or even by spitting.

AND WORST OF ALL . . .

Of all the hardships southern women faced, perhaps the lack of news was the hardest. They never knew from one day to the next where their men were or whether they were alive, dead, or wounded. Some women could not stand the stress. According to Mary Chesnut, "Grief and constant anxiety kill nearly as many women as men die on the battlefield."

Louise Wigfall Wright, who was the daughter of a Confederate senator, Louis Wigfall, described southern

women giving up their men in her dramatic poem
"Requiescat in Pace":

> And we wept, and watched, and waited
> > By our lonely household fire,
> For the mother gave her first born,
> > And the daughter gave her sire!
> And the wife sent forth her husband,
> > And the maiden her lover sweet;
> And our hearts kept time in the silence
> > To the rhythmic tread of their feet.

Chapter Three
Caring for the Wounded

The role that American women played in taking care of the sick and wounded during the Civil War had a lot to do with an Englishwoman. Florence Nightingale was born into a wealthy family. She defied tradition by choosing not to marry but instead to care for sick and wounded people. Previously, female nurses had been poor women without skills who often cared little for their patients.

Nightingale trained as a nurse at a convent in Germany and was running a hospital in London when the Crimean War started. In 1854, she led a group of Englishwomen she had trained to the Crimean Peninsula on the Black Sea, where they took care of the wounded and organized medical care. Nightingale returned to England a heroine and founder of the new profession of nursing for women.

In 1859 she published a book called *Notes on Nursing*. Many American women read it and followed its principles. They were ready to be nurses when the Civil War started. Writer Agatha Young said of Nightingale, "It is possible that the frail little invalid with the sharp nose and acid tongue, lying on her couch in London, may have been the most influential woman of the war."

Florence Nightingale's experiences of wartime nursing in Europe helped the women of the American Civil War.

THE FIRST STEPS

As soon as the war started, women in towns everywhere got together to make uniforms and to cut, sew, and roll fabric to be used as bandages.

Other women went to care for the wounded. Writer Louisa May Alcott's first experience with the wounded was with soldiers from the Battle of Fredericksburg, who arrived in Washington, D.C., by ambulance. She did everything in her ward from washing wounds to serving meals to singing to weeping men who couldn't sleep. After only six weeks, she was sent home suffering from typhoid fever caught from a patient. In 1863, she published *Hospital Sketches* about her experiences.

The men who were sent to such city hospitals would probably first have been treated in a field hospital, a temporary facility near the scene of battle. Sometimes there was not even a building. Instead, the men were laid on the streets to wait their turn for attention. At other times, such as at Gettysburg, the Union had well-organized rows of hundreds of tents prepared for their work. Inside the tents, however, there was nothing wonderful about the work. Limbs were cut off with nothing more than whiskey to drown the pain. There were no medicines that could stop infections. And often there wasn't even enough food.

UNITED STATES SANITARY COMMISSION

In July 1861, the federal government established the United States Sanitary Commission. This was done at the urging of such prominent women as Dr. Elizabeth Blackwell, the first woman in the United States to earn a medical degree. It was a civilian organization that was to assist the Union army in any way it could. It functioned through a vast network of women and men in more than seven thousand local soldiers' aid societies. The local groups collected supplies, shipped them where they were needed, inspected military hospitals, persuaded neighbors to donate money, utilized donations efficiently, and arranged for nursing care for the wounded.

When the war started, the U.S. Army had few doctors and no plans for taking care of the wounded. Even as the war went on, many of the doctors were in their positions purely for political reasons, not for their medical or organizational skills. When women volunteers of the Sanitary Commission came into a hospital camp run by such doctors, the men usually resented their presence.

One of the many stations of the U.S. Sanitary Commission, which oversaw medical facilities, provided nursing care, and distributed items made and purchased by volunteers

The women carried on the work that needed doing without permission or help.

Mary Ann Bickerdyke of Illinois zoomed past such organizational obstacles. Carrying donated money to Cairo, Illinois, she found total filth and disorganization in the military hospital. She moved in and took charge, getting the men cleaned, providing food, and helping wherever she could. Once, when a snarling doctor

Mary Ann Bickerdyke of Illinois, called "Mother" Bickerdyke by the thousands of soldiers she nursed from nineteen different battles

asked where her authority came from, Bickerdyke replied, "On the authority of Lord God Almighty. Have you anything that outranks that?"

As an official representative of the Sanitary Commission, "Mother" Bickerdyke followed General Grant's army for the next four years. She served at the scene of nineteen different battles, more than any other woman. As fighting slowed down during the night, she often scoured the battlefields looking for wounded men lying among the dead.

Most women did not follow the army. But their housekeeping skills kept disease down, their meal-planning skills kept nutrition up, and they made sure

Women selling homemade and donated items at a sanitary commission fair to raise funds for Union soldiers

that men who recovered quickly got back to fighting.

Women all over sent parcels of clothing—and sometimes food—to the sanitary commissions nearest their homes. In 1863, when the Chicago Sanitary Commission ran out of funds to pay for distributing the parcels, Mary Livermore and her colleagues raised funds by holding a

"A SANITARY COMMISSION OF ONE"

Clara Barton was a Massachusetts woman who never wanted to settle down. After teaching for a while, she moved to Washing-ton, D.C., where she talked the Patent Office into hiring her—the first woman to be permanently hired for government work. Her major skill was organizing, and her major emotion was compassion.

When the first military skirmishes took place near Washington, Barton went to see if she could help. She found ex-students of hers lying in filth, with no one caring for their wounds. She and friends took care of the men as best they could, replaced their supplies, wrote letters for them, and brought meals. Soon people all over began sending Barton supplies and money.

After the Battle of Antietam in September 1862, Barton was the first nurse to appear on the scene. She spent hours digging bullets out of hundreds of wounded men. That night, though exhausted, she made nourishing soup for the men.

Barton worked throughout the war at supplying and nursing northern soldiers along the East Coast, often using her own money. She never joined the official system because she felt it was too wasteful and too disorganized.

giant fair. They sold items and livestock donated by people from all over the Midwest. The fair occupied six huge buildings, and the women earned more than $100,000.

Hearing of the success in Chicago, women of other sanitary commissions began to hold fairs of their own. One New York fair took in $2 million.

MISS DIX'S ARMY NURSES

The Union army organized women to serve in hospitals before the Confederates did. As their superintendent, the northern army chose Dorothea Dix. In 1861, the 59-year-old woman was already famous for her work in

Reformer and superintendent of Union nurses Dorothea Dix

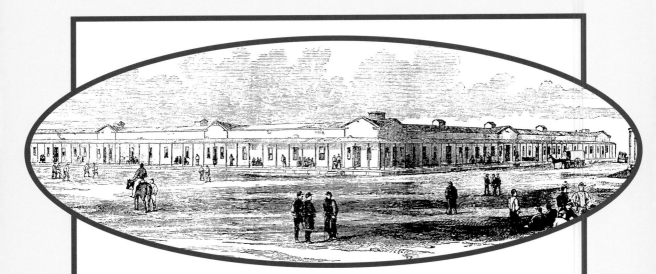

A Union hospital built at Hilton Head, South Carolina

improving conditions in mental hospitals. She insisted that only those women who were plain in appearance and over thirty years old be allowed to serve as nurses. This stern—and often sour—woman had no place in her plans for women who thought it would be "romantic" to serve the wounded. She found more than three thousand women to work for her.

Unfortunately, Dorothea Dix had more good intentions than skills to organize the hospital work. If she found volunteer nurses in a hospital she visited, she tried to force the army doctor in charge to dismiss them, no matter how badly they were needed.

Two nursing efforts went on throughout the war—one under the control of the military, with Dorothea Dix in charge, and one run by civilian women who often had a better sense of how to get things done. Because she was later dissatisfied with the results of her war work, Dix hoped that she would be judged by her other accomplishments.

THE DOCTOR

At least one woman is known to have served as a military physician during the Civil War. She was Mary Walker, who attended Syracuse Medical College about five years after Elizabeth Blackwell became the first woman to receive a medical degree in the United States.

When the war started, Mary Walker was unable to get any army officials to take seriously her request to serve. She volunteered at tent hospitals in Virginia and then in Tennessee. Finally, in September 1863, she was given an official appointment as an army doctor. Captured by the Confederates the following spring, the woman who usually wore men's clothes was freed in a prisoner exchange. At war's end, she became the only woman to receive a Congressional Medal of Honor.

A woman in a small cottage prepares food for a soldier.

IN THE SOUTH

Southern women had no such thing as a Sanitary Commission. Individual women did what they could to help their fighting men.

Kate Cumming of Alabama went to Corinth, Mississippi, after a battle there. After inspecting the disorganized hospital tents, she wrote, "I do not think that words are in our vocabulary expressive enough to present to the mind the realities of that sad scene." Men who caught the notice of a woman bringing food from town might get fed. The others went hungry.

Sally L. Tompkins turned an old Richmond, Virginia, mansion into a hospital after the First Battle of Bull Run (also called Manassas). When other private hospitals were closed because they charged for their services, which were inadequate anyway, Tompkins's hospital was allowed to stay open. She did such a good job running it (and paying for it) that Confederate President Jefferson Davis made her a captain of cavalry—an "honor" that put her hospital under official control. She was the only Confederate woman to hold an official army commission.

Soldiers received care wherever they could. These women are nursing wounded men in the attic of their home.

"A ward of whitewashed walls"
meant death for many and recuperation for others.

Ella King Newsom of Arkansas volunteered to serve as an apprentice in the hospital in Memphis, Tennessee, so that she could be useful during the war. In December 1861, she worked among the wounded at Bowling Green, Kentucky. She impressed General Albert Sidney Johnston, who made her superintendent of hospitals.

The largest military hospital in the world was Chimborazo Hospital in Richmond. It was administered in five divisions. Phoebe Yates Pember of South Carolina became the nursing administrator of one of the divisions, which consisted of thirty-one fifty-patient buildings. Resentful male administrators often made her work more difficult than it had to be. She later wrote, "A woman must soar beyond the conventional modesty considered correct under different circumstances."

All of Pember's work and responsibility brought in a salary too small to sustain her. At night she ignored her exhaustion and wrote articles to earn extra money.

Marie Ravenel de la Coste of Georgia wrote a song, originally published anonymously, that brought tears to the eyes of all who heard it. Called "Somebody's Darling," it began:

> Into a ward of the whitewashed walls
>> Where the dead and the dying lay—
> Wounded by bayonets, shells, and ball—
>> Somebody's darling was borne one day.
> Somebody's darling! So young and so brave,
>> Wearing still on his pale sweet face—
> Soon to be hid by the dust of the grave—
>> The lingering light of his boyhood's grace.

Chapter Four

"The Country Needed Men"

Women looking for adventure, work, and perhaps romance have always sought the company of soldiers. In the American Civil War, women were among the large number of civilians, called camp followers, who moved around with armies, usually hoping to make money in some way.

Some were present officially, such as women employed to cook or do laundry. At least two thousand such employees of the Union army were ex-slaves, both legally freed and runaway. Other women were unofficial companions, such as those who hoped to become the mistresses of soldiers.

Officers' wives were often allowed to go to an army encampment, and some brought their children. They would move back to the nearest towns or go home when the troops moved into battle. Other women just followed their men, whether they had permission or not. Still others, especially in the North, disguised themselves and became true soldiers.

DAUGHTERS OF THE REGIMENTS

Women often accompanied army regiments as combination nurse and mascot. They were called *vivandières* (which literally means "food supplier" in French) or "daughters of the regiment." They often carried their regiments' flags in parades. One Massachusetts regiment named Clara Barton its "daughter" and gave a full dress parade in her honor.

Kady Brownell of Rhode Island, who had been raised on army bases as the daughter of a Scottish soldier, joined her husband in training and became a sharpshooter and fierce swordswoman. She was named flagbearer for her husband's company. She first saw action at the First Battle of Bull Run on July 21, 1861. Two years later, she was still with the company at the Battle of New Berne, where her husband was wounded. They returned home to Rhode Island together when he was discharged. Though she never told her own story, an account written soon after the war credits Kady with saving

Kady Brownell, sharpshooter and flagbearer

Marie Tebe, a true vivandière

her 5th Rhode Island company by raising her flag through the smoke and dust to prevent other Union regiments from mistaking them for the enemy.

The 2nd Michigan Volunteer Infantry was accompanied by Anna Etheridge, who rode side-saddle right into the middle of a skirmish just before Bull Run. When the action ended, she took bandages from her saddlebags and set up a nursing station. In later actions, she frequently rushed onto a battlefield to rescue wounded men from the midst of the fighting.

Marie Tebe of Pennsylvania, known as "French Mary," was given pay and a fancy uniform by her regiment. A real vivandière, she acted as a supplier to her regiment, finding them liquor and special treats. She also nursed the wounded, mended clothing, and cooked. She herself was wounded at least once and often found new bullet holes in her skirts. She was given a medal after the Battle of Chancellorsville for ignoring flying bullets to give water to the hot and thirsty soldiers.

Irish-born Bridget Divers followed her husband's 1st Michigan Cavalry regiment. Instead of becoming a vivandière, she started working as a nurse and also

A soldier's wife heating cannonballs

became renowned for her bravery in rescuing fallen men from the middle of battle. After the war, "Irish Biddy" joined the U.S. Army as a laundress.

In the Confederate army, the women who accompanied the troops were acceptable only if they seemed "motherly" or were following their husbands into battle. Otherwise, they were regarded as being "loose" women and not respectable.

"HALF-SOLDIER HEROINES"

More than four hundred women are known to have gone to war as actual soldiers. Many more may have served without being identified. Most who were identified as women were discovered only after they were killed or wounded. One author called these women "half-soldier heroines."

Perhaps the longest-serving woman was Irish-born Jennie Hodgers of Illinois, who fought as "Albert Cashier" through the whole war and then lived as Cashier the rest of her life. She was not identified as a woman until she was injured in an automobile accident in 1911. She persuaded the doctor to keep her secret. He helped her get admitted to an old soldiers' home for care. In old age, when asked why she joined the army, she replied, "The country needed men, and I wanted excitement."

WOMAN WITH A STRATEGY

Anna Ella Carroll of Maryland was an avid supporter of the Union. She wrote widely distributed pamphlets reinforcing the opinion that southern secession was unconstitutional. Even more intriguing, however, is the plan

SARAH/FRANK,
SOLDIER AND SPY

S arah Emma Edmonds, a Canadian, ran away from home
and lived as "Franklin Thompson" in Connecticut before
the war. She was living in Michigan when war broke out, and
she joined the 2nd Michigan Volunteer Infantry as a male

nurse and courier. Well known for her riding and shooting skills, she also served as a spy, once even disguising herself as African-American to get admitted to a Confederate army camp. Another time she actively served in the Confederate cavalry. Sarah/Frank deserted the army when the man she loved resigned. She returned to being a woman and lived in Ohio. She later wrote a popular book of memoirs, called *Nurse and Spy in the Union Army*. She admitted that not all her action-packed stories were "strictly" true, but they came very close.

she sent to the War Department showing how the Union could capture the South by invading through the Tennessee River Valley. This is, in fact, what happened.

After the war, Carroll claimed payment for her military strategy, but she acknowledged that the idea was basically that of a riverboat pilot. She was given a small payment, though nothing like the "outrageous" amount she had claimed. When she died in 1894, her tombstone was inscribed: "A great humanitarian and a close friend of Abraham Lincoln."

DEATH AT GETTYSBURG

Only one woman died during Gettysburg, the great three-day battle from which the South never recovered. She wasn't a soldier—she was a housewife doing her baking. Jennie Wade was in her farmhouse in the Pennsylvania countryside when Union soldiers passed by. She willingly baked bread for them, not realizing that they were being pushed on by the Confederates. A southern officer ordered her to stop baking. She ignored him, continuing with her task, when a stray bullet struck her in the head. Her death was hardly noticed as fifty thousand men were killed or wounded around her.

SOUTHERN SOLDIERS

One female Union soldier who was in the army for a year or more was injured and captured at the Battle of Chickamauga. When the Confederate surgeon discovered she was a woman, he sent her back across the lines carrying a message: "As the Confederates do not use women in war, this woman, wounded in battle, is returned to you." The surgeon did not know there were, in fact, women soldiers in the Confederate army.

Amy Clarke, for example, put on men's clothes and enlisted with her husband. After he was killed at the Battle of Shiloh in April 1862, she remained with her regiment until she was wounded and captured. The Union captors ordered her to put on a dress, and they returned her to the Confederates.

Probably the most famous of the few Confederate half-soldiers who have been identified was Loreta Janeta Velazquez, who served under the name of "Harry Buford" with false mustache and beard. A Cuban who was raised in New Orleans, Louisiana, she had decided as a girl that Joan of Arc, the fifteenth-century French soldier and saint, was her heroine.

At the First Battle of Bull Run, "Harry" discovered that

*Loreta Janeta Velazquez
shown in her disguise as
Harry Buford*

"the fiercer the conflict grew the more my courage rose."
She also served in the detective corps but was briefly
imprisoned when found to be a woman. Attaching her
false mustache again, she joined another regiment until
she was wounded.

Sometimes Velazquez dressed as a woman and sometimes as a man. She wore a gown when she married an
officer that she had known before the war. The two of

them had worked together side by side while she was dressed as Lieutenant Buford, but he had failed to recognize her. Soon after their marriage, her husband died in a Union prison. She joined the secret service, working in the North to try to free Confederate prisoners.

FEMALE SPIES

Adventurous southern women served as spies and couriers when the "enemy" was in their own territory. Most such women were certain that their gender would protect them from punishment if caught. But those women who were caught were imprisoned, both by the Confederacy and the Union.

Before the war, as southern states seceded from the Union, southern hostesses in Washington, D.C., headed either back home or to the new confederate capital. Staying behind in Washington was Rose O'Neal Greenhow—enthusiastic hostess and spy.

At her parties, where everyone was welcome, she learned all she could of Union plans and then conveyed the information in code to General Pierre Beauregard, a Confederate commander. Before the First Battle of Bull Run in July 1861, she sent messenger Betty Duvall out

Rose O'Neal Greenhow, with her daughter,
while being held in the Old Capitol Prison

of Washington in a farm cart with the message hidden inside the curls on her head. Because of the information Greenhow sent, the southern army moved up toward Manassas in time to achieve the first great Confederate victory.

As she left her house one day, Greenhow was arrested by Allan Pinkerton, Abraham Lincoln's own detective. She had only an instant to swallow the message she was carrying. She was imprisoned, first in her own house, where she kept up her spying and reporting. After six months, she was moved to the Old Capitol Prison, where the record book listed her as "a dangerous, skillful spy." She spent a bleak year during which she wrote, "Hope paints no silver lining to the clouds which hang over me." After her release, she moved to England and published a book, *My Imprisonment and the First Year of Abolition Rule in Washington.*

Rose Greenhow sailed back toward America with letters and money for the Confederates. Her boat capsized near Cape Fear, North Carolina. Weighed down by gold and her heavy skirts, she drowned. She was buried with military honors.

SPIES FOR THE NORTH

Elizabeth Van Lew was a Virginia woman who had been educated in Philadelphia, where she learned to dislike slavery. Living in Richmond, Virginia, the Confederate capital, she spoke openly in favor of the North. Her neighbors regarded her as silly and called her "Crazy Bett." That opinion of her neighbors kept her from being suspected as she traveled around the city, visited prisons, carried secret messages for the Union army, and even helped Union prisoners escape.

Bett and her mother had freed their own slaves before the war, but those African-Americans who stayed with her as hired servants helped her in her missions. One of them took a job as a servant in the home of Jefferson Davis, president of the Confederacy, where she eavesdropped on rebel officers. Van Lew used up her own funds helping the Union cause, and President Grant later appointed her postmistress of Richmond, to the dismay of her neighbors.

Pauline Cushman was a northern actress who gave shows for the Confederate army—and passed along to the Union whatever she learned from her admirers. Caught with secret papers, she was about to be executed when Union troops overran the position and freed her.

As with "half-soldier heroines," not all female spies and couriers were identified. Some early writers in the decades right after the war suggested that "hundreds" of southern women moved across the lines carrying messages. Perhaps many patriotic women working for South and North made exciting and fearful contributions to the war effort that they kept secret the rest of their lives.

REBEL SPY

Young Belle Boyd of Martinsburg, Virginia (now West Virginia), was a seventeen-year-old debutante with much charm. She became a courier, carrying messages between various Confederate camps. She befriended Union soldiers and sent messages to the Southerners about what she had learned. Her most dangerous, and most famous, exploit occurred in May 1862. She had news that the Union planned to blow up bridges to prevent General Stonewall Jackson from reaching Front Royal. She ran on foot across fields and along streams, evading the fire of sentries who shot at anything that moved, to let Jackson know.

Boyd was arrested at least six times and imprisoned twice. After she was released from Old Capitol Prison in Washington, General Jackson himself warned her that he would probably have to retreat from Martinsburg. This would leave her home vulnerable to seizure by the Union and lead to her own arrest. She moved to Winchester, where Jackson apparently commissioned her as a captain. Although she was helpful to the Confederacy, she scandalized most southerners by her unladylike behavior.

Chapter Five

When the War Ended . . .

More than 600,000 people died in the American Civil War. Many women found themselves widows with no income. They were expected to give up their wartime jobs when soldiers returned. The following years are filled with reports of requests by widows of brave soldiers or even of women soldiers themselves seeking pensions from the government.

Some women did not know whether they were widows or not. Many soldiers were buried, unidentified, in mass graves after battles or in enemy prisons.

Clara Barton realized that some effort must be made to let women know the status of their men. Using her own money and time, she began to search for missing men. President Lincoln announced that she was doing this work, and within weeks she had received thousands upon thousands of requests to locate missing husbands, fathers, and sons. She supported her work by lecturing about the war as she moved around the countryside, investigating graves and prisons.

She published lists of the missing, hoping that others would recognize the names and let her know their fates. She kept up this work for more than four years, identifying more than twenty thousand missing men.

The search for a loved one . . . ended

Barton later traveled to Europe and learned of the International Committee of the Red Cross, which had been started in 1863 by Jean-Henri Dunant of Switzerland. He sought fair treatment for prisoners and wounded in wartime. Barton founded and built up the American Red Cross, which carried on the work she did during the Civil War. It continues today, helping people in war and during natural disasters.

FIFTY YEARS OF ADVANCEMENT

When Clara Barton spoke in public, she told women audiences that because of their work during the war, the American woman was "fifty years in advance of the normal position which continued peace and existing conditions would have assigned her." She said that the women of North and South had disproved the long-held opinion that "women are well enough in their places—wives and mothers and nurses at home—kind and tender but weak and unreliable and worth nothing in an emergency."

Before the war, the women's rights movement had just taken its first steps. The first meeting to discuss the subject was held in 1848 in Seneca Falls, New York. As the war started, most men and many women were still shocked at the idea that women would get together to demand changes.

By the end of the war, many American women had learned that they could take control of their own lives. They had learned that they could work together to accomplish a goal. Soon after the war, some women began running businesses, doing jobs once done only by men. Often they took control of their own money. Eventually they voted in national elections. Women began to view themselves in a new light. Never again would they go back to being the "weaker sex."

MAJOR EVENTS OF THE CIVIL WAR

1860
December 20 South Carolina is the first southern state to secede from the Union.

1861
February 4 Representatives from the seceding states meet in Montgomery, Alabama, and form the Confederate States of America.

February 18 Jefferson Davis, previously U.S. Secretary of War, is inaugurated as president of the Confederate States.

April 12 War begins at 4:30 A.M.. by a Confederate attack on Union-held Fort

April 15 President Abraham Lincoln calls for 75,000 volunteers to help stop the war with the Confederacy.

April 19 Lincoln orders a naval blockade of southern seaports.

July 21 The First Battle of Bull Run (or Manassas) in Virginia is the first important battle; it is won by Confederate troops.

August 10 The Battle of Wilson's Creek in Missouri, another Confederate victory, brings lands west of the Mississippi into the war.

1862
February 16 The fall of Fort Donelson in Tennessee to General Ulysses S. Grant's Union troops opens up Nashville to capture; Nashville becomes the first southern city to be taken by the North.

March 9 The first battle of ironclad ships, the *Monitor* and the *Merrimack* (called the *Virginia* by the Confederacy), ends in a draw but revolutionizes naval warfare.

April 25 New Orleans, Louisiana, is captured by a fleet under the command of David Farragut.

September 4 General Robert E. Lee's Confederate troops move into Maryland, invading the North for the first time and heading toward Pennsylvania.

September 17 Lee's advance is stopped by the Battle of Antietam (or Sharpsburg) in Maryland, in the war's bloodiest day of fighting.

1863
January 1 The Emancipation Proclamation is signed, granting freedom to all slaves within the seceded states.

March 3 The U.S. Congress approves the conscription, or draft, of all able-bodied males between the ages of 20 and 45.

May The first all–African-American regiment in the Union army, the 54th Massachusetts, begins serving.

June 3 Lee begins another advance into the North.

June 9 The Battle of Brandy Station in Virginia turns into the largest cavalry action of the War; the North is forced to retreat.

July 1–3	The Battle of Gettysburg in Pennsylvania ends Lee's attempt to take the North. From this time on, the Confederates fight a defensive battle within their own states.
July 4	The siege of Vicksburg, Mississippi, ends in a Union victory.
July 8	Port Hudson, Louisiana, surrenders, effectively cutting the Confederacy in half as the Union takes control of the entire Mississippi River.
July 13–16	Riots in New York City protesting the draft kill or injure hundreds.
November 19	President Lincoln delivers the Gettysburg Address as a dedication of the national cemetery at Gettysburg, Pennsylvania.

1864

March 10	General Grant is put in charge of the entire U.S. Army.
August 5	The Battle of Mobile Bay in Alabama is won by the Union fleet under Admiral Farragut.
September 1	The Union army, under General William T. Sherman, captures Atlanta, Georgia.
October 19	After more than two months of fighting in the Shenandoah Valley of Virginia, General Philip Sheridan's cavalry regiments take the valley in the Battle of Cedar Creek, leaving the Confederates without an important source of food or a place to regroup.
November	General Sherman's army marches the 300 miles (483 km) from Atlanta to the Atlantic Ocean, living off the land and destroying everything the Confederates might find useful.

1865

March 13	Out of desperation, the Confederate Congress votes to recruit African-American soldiers. Five days later, the Confederate Congress no longer exists.
April 2	Richmond, Virginia, the capital of the Confederacy, falls to the Union.
April 9	Lee surrenders to Grant at Appomatox Court House in Virginia.
April 14	Abraham Lincoln is shot by southern sympathizer John Wilkes Booth. He dies the next day.
December 18	The Thirteenth Amendment to the Constitution, abolishing slavery, goes into effect.

FOR MORE INFORMATION

FOR FURTHER READING

Hakim, Joy. *War, Terrible War*. A History of US, Book Six. New York: Oxford University Press, 1994.

Durwood, Thomas A., et al. *The History of the Civil War*. 10 vols. New York: Silver Burdett, 1990.

Tracey, Patrick. *Military Leaders of the Civil War*. American Profiles series. New York: Facts on File, 1993.

VIDEOS

The Civil War. 9 vols. Produced by Ken Burns. PBS Home Video.
The Civil War. 2 vols. Pied Piper.

CD-ROMS

African-American History—Slavery to Civil Rights. Queue.
American Heritage Civil War CD. Simon & Schuster Interactive.
Civil War: Two Views CD. Clearvue.
Civil War—America's Epic Struggle. 2 CD set. Multi-Educator.

INTERNET SITES

Due to the changeable nature of the Internet, sites appear and disappear very quickly. The resources listed below offered useful information on the Civil War at the time of publication. Internet addresses must be entered with capital and lowercase letters exactly as they appear.

The Yahoo directory of the World Wide Web is an excellent place to find Internet sites on any topic. The directory is located at:
http://www.yahoo.com

The Internet has hundreds of sites with information about the Civil War. The United States Civil War Center at Louisiana State University maintains a Web site for the gathering and sharing of information:
http://www.cwc.lsu.edu

The Civil War in Miniature, by R. L. Curry, is a collection of documented facts and interesting tidbits that brings many of the different facets of the Civil War together:
http://serve.aeneas.net/ais/civwamin/

The National Park Service maintains sites on hundreds of Civil War battles. The directory of these sites is at:
http://www.cv.nps.gov/abpp/battles/camp.html

Many sites reproduce primary documents related to the Civil War. Duke University maintains a site about women in the Civil War that contains, among other things, a biography of Rose O'Neil Greenhow based on documents collected at the University; this site also provides links to other organizations with information on women in the Civil War:
http://scriptorium.lib.duke.edu/collections/civil-war-women.html

INDEX

About the Author

Jean F. Blashfield is a writer with more than fifty books to her credit. Most of them are for young people, covering many subjects from chemistry to women inventors to England to World War II. She also has written several fantasy adventure stories and retold the stories of Gilbert and Sullivan operettas. She developed the American Civil War series for Franklin Watts with her husband, Wallace B. Black.

A graduate of the University of Michigan, Ms. Blashfield has been a book editor for many years. She developed three encyclopedias for young people, wrote educational materials about space for NASA, and created the Awesome Almanacs of various states for her own publishing company.

DATE DUE
